anythink

D1442285

Arctic Animals
Life Outside the Igloo

Collared Lemming

by Dee Phillips

Consultants:

Dominique Fauteux
Department of Biology, Laval University, Quebec, Canada

Kimberly Brenneman, PhD
National Institute for Early Education Research, Rutgers University, New Brunswick, New Jersey

BEARPORT
PUBLISHING

New York, New York

Credits

Cover, © Andrey Zvoznikov/Ardea; 2–3, © J. L. Klein and M. L. Hubert/FLPA; 4, © Incredible Arctic/Shutterstock; 5, © J. L. Klein and M. L. Hubert/FLPA; 7, © Christine Lambert; 8, © Andrey Zvoznikov/Ardea; 9, © J. L. Klein and M. L. Hubert/FLPA, © PavelSvoboda/Shutterstock, © Igor Janicek/Shutterstock, © AlenKadr/Shutterstock, and © Potapov Alexander/Shutterstock; 10, © David Hosking/FLPA; 11, © J. L. Klein and M. L. Hubert/FLPA; 12T, © Alaska Stock/Superstock; 12B, © Matthias Breiter/Minden Pictures/FLPA; 13, © Andrius Vaicikonis/Shutterstock; 15, © Andrey Zvoznikov/Ardea; 16, © J. L. Klein and M. L. Hubert/FLPA; 17, © Tom McHugh/Science Photo Library; 18, © J. L. Klein and M. L. Hubert/FLPA; 19, © Christine Lambert; 21, © Tom McHugh/Science Photo Library; 23TC, © J. L. Klein and M. L. Hubert/FLPA; 23TR, © Christine Lambert; 23BL, © J. L. Klein and M. L. Hubert/FLPA; 23BC, © Erni/Shutterstock; 23BR, © Gregory A. Pozhvanov/Shutterstock.

Publisher: Kenn Goin
Creative Director: Spencer Brinker
Editor: Jessica Rudolph
Photo Researcher: Ruby Tuesday Books Ltd

Library of Congress Cataloging-in-Publication Data

Phillips, Dee, 1967– author.
  Collared lemming / by Dee Phillips.
      pages cm. — (Arctic animals : life outside the igloo)
  Includes bibliographical references and index.
  ISBN 978-1-62724-528-9 (library binding) — ISBN 1-62724-528-6 (library binding)
  1. Collared lemming—Juvenile literature. 2. Lemmings—Juvenile literature. 3. Arctic regions—Juvenile literature. I. Title.
  QL737.R666.P45 2015
  599.35'82—dc23
                              2014041318

For more information, write to Bearport Publishing Company, Inc., 45 West 21st Street, Suite 3B, New York, New York 10010. Printed in the United States of America.

10 9 8 7 6 5 4 3 2 1

Contents

Cozy Under the Snow

It's fall in one of the coldest places on Earth—the **Arctic**.

The ground is covered in thick snow.

It looks like there are no animals around.

However, beneath the snow, a collared lemming rests in its cozy **burrow**.

There, the small, furry creature is protected from the freezing Arctic weather.

the Arctic

Collared lemmings belong to a group of animals called rodents. This group includes mice, rats, and hamsters.

a collared lemming
under the snow

An Arctic Home

The collared lemming's Arctic home is in the most northern part of the world.

In the Arctic, temperatures can drop to −40°F (−40°C).

Lemmings live on a kind of land called **tundra**.

This flat, rocky land is buried under ice and snow for most of the year.

No trees grow on the tundra, and only a few tough plants can survive there.

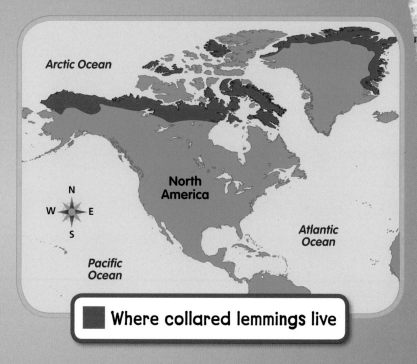

Arctic Ocean

North America

Atlantic Ocean

Pacific Ocean

N W E S

Where collared lemmings live

Digging a Burrow

In winter, a lemming survives in the freezing Arctic by spending most of its time below the snow's surface.

It uses its long claws to dig burrows.

First, the lemming digs a short tunnel into the snow or ice.

Then, at the end of the tunnel, it digs a small room.

It fills the room with dry grass.

This is where the lemming rests and sleeps.

a lemming's claws

A lemming may dig several burrows each winter. It also digs many long tunnels under the snow that connect one burrow to another.

Arctic tundra

entrance to burrow

thick snow

tunnel

small room

tunnel to another burrow

soil

Searching for Food

In winter, collared lemmings eat twigs from bushes called arctic willows.

These bushes often get buried under the snow.

To search for twigs, lemmings dig many long snow tunnels.

As they scurry along the tunnels, the lemmings find twigs to gobble up.

arctic willow

During winter, lemmings keep warm by living under the ice and snow. There's also another reason why lemmings stay under the snow. What do you think this could be?

In summer, it gets a little warmer in the Arctic. Many plants grow for just a few weeks. During this time, lemmings eat the leaves and shoots of arctic willows. They also eat flowers, berries, and grass.

a collared lemming eating flowers in summer

Hiding from Enemies

Living under the snow and ice helps lemmings hide from **predators**.

Arctic foxes, wolves, weasels, and owls all hunt lemmings.

Collared lemmings aren't always safe under the snow, however.

Arctic foxes listen for the sound of lemmings moving in their tunnels.

Then the foxes jump up, dive into the snow, and try to grab the little lemmings.

an arctic fox hunting a lemming

weasel

Weasels have long, thin bodies. They are able to get inside a lemming's tunnels and hunt for the animal.

Collared lemmings try to hide from predators in tunnels and burrows. They also have another way to keep safe in winter. What do you think this could be?

A White Coat for Winter

During winter, collared lemmings grow thick coats of white fur.

This helps to protect them. How?

Sometimes lemmings have to come to the surface to look for food.

Their white coats help them blend in with the snowy surroundings.

As a result, it's hard for foxes and other predators to see them.

A collared lemming has thick fur on the bottom of its paws. It also has long, stiff hairs that stick out from between its toes. The fur and hairs keep the lemming from slipping on ice and snow.

In winter, lemmings dig burrows in snow and ice. In summer, the snow and ice melt. Where do you think lemmings live during this time of year?

Warmer Days

When spring arrives in the Arctic, the weather gets a little warmer.

The ice and snow begin to melt, but lemmings don't stop digging.

Now they dig new burrows and long tunnels—in the soil.

The lemmings use their summer burrows and tunnels for resting and hiding from predators.

a lemming in a tunnel in the soil

In spring, a female lemming digs a special room in one of her burrows. What do you think she uses this room for?

In spring, collared lemmings lose their white winter coats and grow new grayish-brown coats. The new fur blends in with rocks on the tundra. This helps the lemmings hide from predators above the ground.

a lemming's summer coat

Little Lemmings

In spring, male and female lemmings find each other and **mate**.

A female lemming then digs a nest room in one of her burrows.

About 20 days after mating, she gives birth to a **litter** of babies in her nest.

A litter may have just one baby lemming or as many as seven.

The newborn lemmings cannot see or hear, and they have no fur.

a mother lemming in her burrow

A female lemming collects grass, bird feathers, and hair from musk oxen that she finds on the tundra. She uses the materials to make a soft bed in the nest room for her babies.

a two-day-old lemming

A newborn collared lemming is tiny. Hold a quarter in your hand. The coin weighs just a little more than a baby lemming!

The Babies Grow Up

Safe in their nest, the baby lemmings drink milk from their mother's body.

After about ten days, they can see and hear and their fur has grown.

A few days later, they start to spend time outside exploring and eating plants.

Then, when they are just three weeks old, the little lemmings can take care of themselves.

They are ready to begin their grown-up lives on the Arctic tundra!

A female collared lemming may have up to five litters of babies in a single year.

If a female lemming gives birth to five litters in one year, and there are five babies in each litter, how many babies in total does she raise that year?

(The answer is on page 24.)

four-week-old collared lemmings

Science Lab

Create a Collared Lemming Poster

Imagine you are a scientist studying collared lemmings. Create a poster that shows how the lemmings live in the freezing Arctic winter.

Read the questions below and think about the answers. You can include this information in your poster.

How do collared lemmings stay protected from the cold weather?

How do lemmings find food?

What predators hunt collared lemmings?

Add labels to your poster. After you are finished, present your poster to your friends and family.

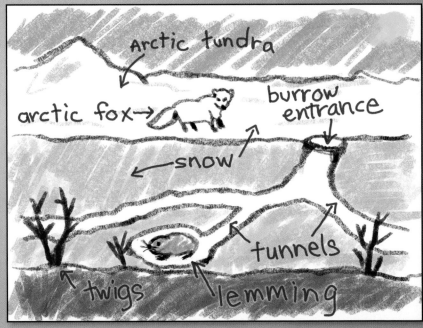

Science Words

Arctic (ARK-tik) the northernmost area on Earth, which includes the Arctic Ocean and the North Pole

burrow (BUR-oh) a hole or tunnel dug by an animal to live in

litter (LIT-ur) a group of animals born to the same mother at the same time

mate (MAYT) to come together in order to have young

predators (PRED-uh-turz) animals that hunt and eat other animals

tundra (TUHN-druh) cold, rocky, treeless land where few plants grow

Index

Read More

Slade, Suzanne. *What If There Were No Lemmings?: A Book About the Tundra Ecosystem (Food Chain Reactions).* Mankato, MN: Picture Window Books (2011).

Squire, Ann. *Lemmings (True Book).* New York: Children's Press (2007).

Learn More Online

To learn more about collared lemmings, visit **www.bearportpublishing.com/ArcticAnimals**

About the Author

Dee Phillips lives near the ocean on the southwest coast of England. She develops and writes nonfiction and fiction books for children of all ages.

Answer for Page 20

The female lemming will give birth to and raise 25 babies that year.